Garfield
Here's Looking At You

JIM DAVIS

RAVETTE BOOKS

First published by Ravette Books Limited 1985
Reprinted 1986, 1987
This edition first published 1988
Reprinted 1989, 1990, 1991, 1993

Printed and bound in Great Britain
for Ravette Books Limited,
8 Clifford Street, London W1X 1RB
An Egmont Company
by Cox & Wyman Ltd, Reading

ISBN 0 906710 74 X

OH, GARFIELD
JIM DAVIS
WHAT HAPPENED TO MY CANDY CARAMELS?
11-11
MON'T MOOK AT MEEF
© 1981 United Feature Syndicate, Inc.

OBOY! PIZZA!
JIM DAVIS
11-6
UH-OH
OKAY, WHO'S IN THERE?
AIN'T NOBODY HERE BUT US ANCHOVIES
© 1981 United Feature Syndicate, Inc.

WHY DON'T WE RUN OUT THERE AND EAT ALL THE FOOD?
MY OWNER WON'T LET US
10-17
JIM DAVIS
THEN LET'S KILL HIM
IT IS NOT WISE TO RUB OUT THE HAND THAT FEEDS YOU
CAN I NIBBLE THE TOES OUT OF HIS SWEAT SOCKS?
© 1981 United Feature Syndicate, Inc.

OH NO! I FEEL A NAP ATTACK COMING ON. BUT THE MOVIE'S ALMOST OVER. I MUST STAY AWAKE!
JIM DAVIS
1-9

Z

DO YOU KNOW WHY I HATE NERMAL?
JIM DAVIS
IT'S NOT BECAUSE HE'S SO YOUNG, TINY AND CUTE...
9-1
HE REMINDS ME I'M SO OLD, FAT AND UGLY
© 1981 United Feature Syndicate, Inc.

WELL IF IT ISN'T NERMAL, THE SHIRLEY TEMPLE OF THE FELINE SET
JIM DAVIS
8-31
HOW'S IT GOING, NERMAL?
OH, ABOUT THE SAME. I'M OVER-ADORED AS USUAL
© 1981 United Feature Syndicate, Inc.

EAT YOUR FOOD, GARFIELD
NO. IT'S YUKKY
JIM DAVIS
2-25
HOW WOULD YOU LIKE TO GO TO BED WITHOUT DINNER?
SOMEHOW, THAT PSYCHOLOGY DOESN'T SEEM TO WORK ON GARFIELD
© 1981 United Feature Syndicate, Inc.

IT'S YAWN AND CRICK TIME
JIM DAVIS
2-24
YAWN
CRICK!
© 1981 United Feature Syndicate, Inc.

BOY, WHAT A GREAT NIGHT'S SLEEP
YAWN
JIM DAVIS
1-10
HEY, GARFIELD. LET'S GO JOGGING
Z
© 1981 United Feature Syndicate, Inc.

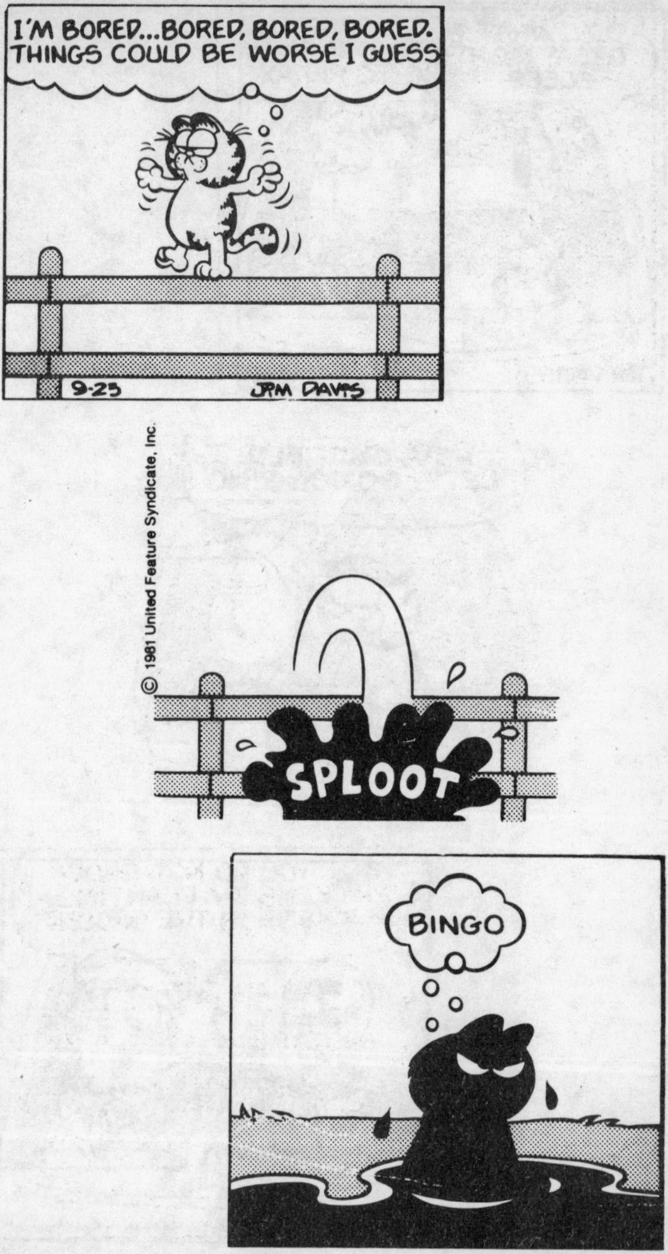
I'M BORED...BORED, BORED, BORED. THINGS COULD BE WORSE I GUESS
9-25
JIM DAVIS
SPLOOT
BINGO

JUST REMEMBER, GARFIELD, WHEN WE GET TO THE FARM YOU ARE THERE TO RELAX
JIM DAVIS
3-30
I KNOW LAST TIME YOU WANTED TO BE HELPFUL...
BUT YOU DO NOT GROW CHICKENS BY PLANTING CHICKENS IN THE GROUND!
IT WAS AN HONEST MISTAKE
© 1981 United Feature Syndicate, Inc.

OUT !
JIM DAVIS
6-2

YOU CAN SCRATCH MY CHAIR,
YOU CAN INSULT MY MOTHER,
YOU CAN BEAT UP MY DOG,
AND YOU CAN PLAY WITH
MY RUBBER MOUSIE...

BUT YOU DON'T
EAT MY FOOD
AND YOU DON'T
SLEEP IN MY BED
YES, SIR

COME HERE, NERMAL
6-4
MAKE YOURSELF USEFUL
JIM DAVIS
WHERE ARE YOU GOING?
TROLLING FOR DOGS
© 1981 United Feature Syndicate, Inc.

HEY, GARFIELD. LET'S SPEND TODAY CELEBRATING ALL THAT'S GOOD IN MANKIND
12-7
JIM DAVIS
LET'S DO A GOOD DEED FOR A STRANGER, STOP AND SMELL A FLOWER AND COMPLIMENT A FRIEND
THAT'S A HEAVY THING TO LAY ON A CAT FIRST THING IN THE MORNING
© 1981 United Feature Syndicate, Inc.

WOULD YOU LIKE TO GO CAMPING, GARFIELD?
JIM DAVIS
WHAT?! AND GET WET WHEN IT RAINS, FREEZE AT NIGHT AND GET THORNS IN MY PAWS?!
WE'LL HAVE PAN-BAKED LASAGNA
I'M PACKED. LET'S GO
5-18

EVERYTHING'S PACKED FOR THE CAMPING TRIP, GARFIELD. DID I FORGET ANYTHING?
JIM DAVIS
ANYTHING ELSE?
YES, 250 MILES OF EXTENSION CORD
5-19

JIM DAVIS
5-20
THERE'S ONLY ONE THING I LIKE ABOUT CARS

THE UPHOLSTERED CEILINGS

BOING
BOING
JIM DAVIS
5-22
ARE YOU BORED, GARFIELD?
HE'LL FIND OUT HOW BORED I AM IF I DON'T GET TO A LITTER BOX SOON

JIM DAVIS
5-21
GARFIELD! GET OUT OF THERE!
THE LIGHT DOES TURN OFF WHEN THE GLOVE COMPARTMENT IS CLOSED
© 1981 United Feature Syndicate, Inc.

GET OUT OF THE CAR, GARFIELD
JIM DAVIS
LET US BASK IN THE SUN AND SLEEP WITH NATURE'S CREATURES, GARFIELD
5-23
TRANSLATION: "LET'S BAKE OUR BRAINS AND LIE ON THE GROUND WITH BUGS AND SNAKES, GARFIELD"
© 1981 United Feature Syndicate, Inc.

COME ON ACROSS THE CREEK, GARFIELD
5-25
JIM DAVIS
I DON'T KNOW WHY YOU CATS ARE SO AFRAID OF A LITTLE MUD
YOU WOULD BE TOO IF YOU HAD TO WASH YOURSELF WITH YOUR TONGUE
© 1981 United Feature Syndicate, Inc.

WELCOME TO OUR FIRST NIGHT OF CAMPING, GARFIELD, ENJOY
5-26
JIM DAVIS
ROAR!
© 1981 United Feature Syndicate, Inc.
YOU ENJOY. I'LL BE WAITING IN THE CAR

LOCK YOUR DOOR, GARFIELD. THIS IS A TOUGH NEIGHBORHOOD
JIM DAVIS
5-27
I KNOW
HOW OFTEN DO YOU SEE KIDS HAVING A FIRE HYDRANT EATING CONTEST?
© 1981 United Feature Syndicate, Inc.

JIM DAVIS
5-28
© 1981 United Feature Syndicate, Inc.

JIM DAVIS
TELL ME THAT'S NOT A TRAFFIC COP'S HAT YOU'RE WEARING, GARFIELD
OKAY, IT'S NOT A TRAFFIC COP'S HAT
5-29
© 1981 United Feature Syndicate, Inc.

I'M BORED. I THINK I'LL STEP OUT FOR SOME FRESH AIR
JIM DAVIS
5-30
GARFIELD! WE ARE GOING OVER 50!
SO I NOTICED

WE CATS NAP ANYWHERE, ANY TIME
JIM DAVIS
1-6
EVERYONE SHOULD BE SO LUCKY
WITH THE POSSIBLE EXCEPTION OF AIRLINE PILOTS
© 1981 United Feature Syndicate, Inc.

I'VE BEEN WATCHING TELEVISION TOO LONG
JIM DAVIS
I'D BETTER TAKE A BREAK
© 1981 United Feature Syndicate, Inc.
1-14

GARFIELD
JIM DAVIS
10-28

ONE STEP CLOSER AND I'LL PUT THAT TONGUE IN A SPLINT
GARFIELD

YOU GOTTA SPEAK THEIR LANGUAGE
GARFIELD

MAYBE I COULD BE AS POPULAR AS NERMAL IF I LEARNED TO DANCE
JIM DAVIS
9-3
I THINK I HURT SOMETHING
© 1981 United Feature Syndicate, Inc.

MINE!
GARFIELD
JIM DAVIS
9-4

GARFIELD

YOURS
GARFIELD

I FEEL LIKE GETTING INTO A BIG FIGHT TODAY
JIM DAVIS
8-6
NOW I FEEL LIKE HOLING UP SOMEWHERE TO WHIMPER FOR A WHILE
© 1981 United Feature Syndicate, Inc

IT'S JUST MY LUCK TO FALL INTO A HOG WALLER
9-24
JIM DAVIS
NOTHING IS LESS APPEALING THAN A MUDDY CAT
© 1981 United Feature Syndicate, Inc.
HELLO THERE, GOOD LOOKIN'
OH SHUT UP

HOW CAN YOU HOGS STAND TO LIE IN A WALLER ALL DAY?
9-25
JIM DAVIS
THE MUD KEEPS THE FLIES OFF AND KEEPS US COOL
© 1981 United Feature Syndicate, Inc
AND IF WE EVER GET OUT, THE MUD DRYS INSTANTLY

IT'S TIME TO GO HOME, GARFIELD. LET ME KNOCK THAT MUD OFF YOU
9-26
© 1981 United Feature Syndicate, Inc.
CRACK!
JIM DAVIS
THANKS... I THINK

HERE IT COMES AGAIN!
JIM DAVIS
1-8
NAP ATTACK!
ZZZZ
© 1981 United Feature Syndicate, Inc.

Z
1-7
JIM DAVIS
Z
© 1981 United Feature Syndicate, Inc.
WHEN GARFIELD NAPS, HE NAPS **HARD**
Z

JIM DAVIS
9-16
HA HA HA!
WHAT A GREAT PLOT, FINE ACTING, SUPER PHOTOGRAPHY
© 1981 United Feature Syndicate, Inc.
I LOVE COMMERCIALS

BRINNNNG!
JIM DAVIS
2·23
I LOVE TO WAKE UP EARLY
THE EARLIER YOU SET YOUR ALARM, THE LONGER YOU CAN OVERSLEEP
© 1981 United Feature Syndicate, Inc.

SLEEP ON MY TEDDY BEAR, WILL YOU?!
Z
JIM DAVIS
12-3
Z
I WISH I COULD DO THAT
Z
© 1981 United Feature Syndicate, Inc.

9-17
JIM DAVIS
YOU'RE NO LONGER A KITTEN, GARFIELD
© 1981 United Feature Syndicate, Inc.

WHAT'S THIS WELLING UP WITHIN MY SOUL?
3-4
JIM DAVIS
BY GOLLY, IT'S MY PRIMAL URGES
CIVILIZATION AS WE KNOW IT MAY COME TO AN END NOW THAT THE **CLAW** IS HERE!
© 1981 United Feature Syndicate, Inc.

THE CLAW SETS OUT TO WREAK HAVOC
JIM DAVIS
3-7
CRASH
BAM
SMASH
WHAM
© 1981 United Feature Syndicate, Inc.
THE CLAW GETS HIS HAVOC WREAKED BY THE FANG

I THINK YOU'RE EATING TOO MUCH SALT, GARFIELD. I'M GOING TO TAKE IT OUT OF YOUR DIET
JIM DAVIS
IF YOU MUST
© 1981 United Feature Syndicate, Inc.
7-20
BUT I'M SURE GOING TO MISS MY SALT LICK
GARFIELD

CLAWS
3-3
JIM DAVIS
THOCK!
THE ONLY WAY TO EAT OLIVES
© 1981 United Feature Syndicate, Inc.

I'M HUNGRY... NAH, I'M TOO TIRED TO BE HUNGRY... NAH, I'M TOO DEPRESSED TO BE TIRED
JIM DAVIS
8-23
YUP
IT'S MONDAY

JIM DAVIS
1-18
GOOD MORNING...
...GARFIELD
CAFFEINE MAKES ME NERVOUS

FOOD, FOOD, FOOD, IS THAT ALL YOU THINK ABOUT, GARFIELD?
THAT'S ABOUT IT
4-14
SO WHAT AM I, CHOPPED LIVER?
© 1982 United Feature Syndicate, Inc.
JIM DAVIS
DON'T FLATTER YOURSELF
HE CERTAINLY KNOWS HOW TO MAKE A GIRL FEEL GOOD

FOLLOW ME, NERMAL. THIS IS HOW YOU CLIMB A TREE
JIM DAVIS
NOW WHAT DO WE DO?
WHAT A SILLY QUESTION
10-20
© 1982 United Feature Syndicate, Inc.
WE SIT HERE UNTIL THE FIRE DEPARTMENT COMES

THIS WEEK I'M GOING TO CHANGE MY WAYS. I'M GOING TO BEGIN BY NO LONGER HATING MONDAYS
JIM DAVIS
9-6
I'M CRAZY ABOUT MONDAYS. I JUST LOVE MONDAYS

NOW I'M ONLY FOND OF MONDAYS

HELLO. WHAT'S THIS?
JIM DAVIS
3-27
DON'T PANIC, GARFIELD. IT'S ONLY A LITTLE RAIN
AAAAAAAAAAAAAA
© 1981 United Feature Syndicate, Inc.

JUST WHAT IS A MONDAY?
JIM DAVIS 5-10
GARFIELD
PLIP
GARFIELD
MONDAY IS A DAY DESIGNED TO ADD DEPRESSION TO AN OTHERWISE HAPPY WEEK

I'M NOT LEAVING BED, I'M NOT MOVING A MUSCLE. IF I DON'T BOTHER MONDAY, MAYBE MONDAY WON'T BOTHER ME
JIM DAVIS
10-18
HELLO, I'M NERMAL, THE WORLD'S CUTEST KITTEN, HERE TO VISIT FOR THE WEEK
WELL, MAYBE I WILL DO JUST A TEENSY BIT OF SOBBING
© 1982 United Feature Syndicate, Inc.

HERE'S HOW TO HANDLE A FIERCE ANIMAL
JIM DAVIS
1-6-82
SHOW NO FEAR
AND SHOW NO PAIN
© 1981 United Feature Syndicate, Inc.

WHAT A DISMAL DAY. I THINK I'LL STAY IN BED ALL DAY
JIM DAVIS
3-8
GOOD MORNING, GARFIELD. IT'S A BEAUTIFUL DAY TODAY
WHAT A BEAUTIFUL DAY. I THINK I'LL STAY IN BED ALL DAY
© 1982 United Feature Syndicate, Inc.

JIM DAVIS
3-6
© 1982 United Feature Syndicate, Inc.

OH, NO!
JiM DAViS
9-13
I AM **DEFINITELY** NOT GETTING OUT OF BED TODAY
NOT ON MONDAY THE 13TH

JIM DAVIS
AHCHOO!
© 1982 United Feature Syndicate, Inc.
3-10
GESUNDHEIT
SNIFF

AND NOW, A WORD FROM OUR SPONSOR
JIM DAVIS
3-11
© 1982 United Feature Syndicate, Inc.
ZOOM
WELCOME BACK

I HATE MONDAY... SOMETHING BAD ALWAYS HAPPENS TO ME ON MONDAY. IT'S JUST A MATTER OF TIME NOW...
JIM DAVIS
8-2

THE SUSPENSE IS KILLING ME

DO IT TO ME NOW, MONDAY! GET IT OVER WITH!

THE MIRROR IS ONE OF CAT'S BEST FRIENDS, NERMAL. YOU CAN PRIMP IN IT, PLAY WITH IT AND ADMIRE YOURSELF IN IT
JIM DAVIS
10-19

I DON'T SEE WHAT'S SO GREAT ABOUT IT

JIM DAVIS
9-17
© 1984 United Feature Syndicate, Inc
IT'S DIET TIME, GARFIELD
I WAS AFRAID OF THAT

JIM DAVIS
RATS, GARFIELD FELL ASLEEP IN THE MIDDLE OF THE FLOOR
9-15
HAVE YOU EVER TRIED TO PICK UP A SLEEPING CAT?
© 1984 United Feature Syndicate, Inc
IT'S IMPOSSIBLE

OH, NO! A FLEA! I'M GETTING YOU A FLEA COLLAR, GARFIELD
LET'S NOT BE TOO HASTY HERE
11-13
LOOK AT THOSE DISTINCTIVE YELLOW AND GREEN MARKINGS THERE
© 1984 United Feature Syndicate, Inc.
THIS FLEA IS A MEMBER OF A RARE SPECIES OF VEGETARIANS
JIM DAVIS

WELL, THERE'S YOUR NEW FLEA COLLAR, GARFIELD
11-14

WAIT A MINUTE, THERE'S A DISCLAIMER ON THIS BOX. "WARNING: WHILE THIS COLLAR WILL REPEL FLEAS..."

"IT HAS BEEN KNOWN TO ATTRACT SHARKS"
JIM DAVIS

DON'T TAKE THAT FLEA COLLAR OFF, GARFIELD!
WHO NEEDS IT?

TUNA
11-15
JIM DAVIS

YOU HAVE A PRETTY GRIM FLEA PROBLEM THERE, ODIE
THAT'S NOT A VERY STRONG FLEA COLLAR
JIM DAVIS 11-16

ONE NICE THING ABOUT CONFIDING IN PETS IS THAT THEY ARE NON-JUDG-MENTAL
JIM DAVIS 9-12
GARFIELD, I GOT A SPEEDING TICKET TODAY
THAT WAS A STUPID THING TO DO
SMACK!
© 1984 United Feature Syndicate,Inc

HEE HEE, THERE'S MORE THAN ONE WAY TO SKIN A CAT
JIM DAVIS 9-14

WHIRRRRR!

HOW PROPHETIC

HOLD IT RIGHT THERE. I ALWAYS WANT TO REMEMBER YOU LIKE THIS
GARF
JIM DAVIS

AS THE KIND, BENEVOLENT PROVIDER
GARF

TRYING TO POISON ME WITH THAT CAT FOOD!
GARFIELD
9-25

GARFIELD! COME HERE!
JIM DAVIS
11-12

"GARFIELD" THIS, "GARFIELD" THAT. I'M SICK OF MY NAME

HEY, FLEABAG! COME HERE!
THEN AGAIN, "GARFIELD" DOES HAVE A CERTAIN RING TO IT

ARE YOU IN THERE, GARFIELD?
JIM DAVIS
9-6
© 1984 United Feature Syndicate, Inc.
THERE AIN'T NOBODY HERE BUT US CHICKENS
I WILL NOT SPEAK TO YOUR RUBBER CHICKEN!
THINK OF STRETCH AS MY SOCIAL SECRETARY

JIM DAVIS 8-13
WHAP!
SOMETIME, SOMEWHERE, WHEN YOU ARE LEAST EXPECTING IT... MONDAY STRIKES
© 1984 United Feature Syndicate, Inc.

JIM DAVIS 8-14
WHAT'S WRONG WITH THIS PICTURE?
GARFIEL
THERE'S NO FOOD IN YOUR BOWL, GARFIELD
GIVE THE MAN A CIGAR! FILL IT UP, TURKEY
GARFIEL
I HATE IT WHEN LOWER LIFE FORMS ARE CONDESCENDING TO ME

I'VE BEEN TAKEN! THERE WAS ONLY ONE KERNEL OF POPCORN IN THIS WHOLE BAG
POP CORN
POP-A-LOT
JIM DAVIS
OH, WELL, ONE'S BETTER THAN NOTHING
POP CORN
POP-A-LOT
POP!
POP-A-LOT
© 1984 United Feature Syndicate, Inc.
8-15

DOC BOY! HOW'S MY FAVORITE LITTLE BROTHER?
JIM DAVIS
11-19
OH, THINGS ARE PRETTY MUCH THE SAME HERE, WILD PARTIES GOOD TIMES, THE USUAL...
UH, YOU SAY YOU'RE COMING TO VISIT?
IT'S PUT UP OR SHUT UP TIME

WHAT AM I GOING TO DO, GARFIELD? MY BROTHER IS COMING TO VISIT FROM THE FARM
JIM DAVIS
11-20
HE THINKS I LIVE LIFE IN THE FAST LANE
"LIFE IN THE PARKING LOT" IS MORE LIKE IT
I DON'T KNOW WHERE HE GOT THE IDEA
IT WAS WHEN YOU TOLD HIM YOU WERE NEGOTIATING MOVIE RIGHTS TO YOUR DIARY
© 1984 United Feature Syndicate, Inc.

THERE'S MY BROTHER NOW
DING DONG
JPM DAVPS 11·21
WELCOME TO THE BIG CITY, DOC BOY! LET THE GOOD TIMES ROLL!
© 1984 United Feature Syndicate, Inc.
ANOTHER SODA POP?
NO. I THINK I'LL HAVE SOME MORE OF THAT FUN-FILLED POPCORN
I'M GOING TO LIKE DOC BOY

I'M SO EMBARRASSED. DOC BOY COMES ALL THE WAY FROM THE FARM JUST TO FIND OUT WHAT A LOSER I AM
THE TRUTH ALWAYS HURTS
11-22
HEY, WHERE ARE ALL THOSE "GOOD TIMES" YOU PROMISED ME?
WHAT WOULD YOU LIKE TO DO?
JIM DAVIS
LET'S GO TO THE AIRPORT AND WATCH THE AIRPLANES LAND
WHATEVER YOU SAY, WILD MAN!
JON JUST GOT OFF THE HOOK
© 1984 United Feature Syndicate, Inc.

OH, BY THE WAY, DOC BOY, I'VE FIXED US UP ON A DOUBLE DATE
HEY, GREAT!
JIM DAVIS 11-23
WHAT'S A DOUBLE DATE?
THAT'S WHEN YOU AND I GO ON A DATE TOGETHER
© 1984 United Feature Syndicate, Inc.
GEE, IT SEEMS LIKE IT WOULD BE MORE FUN IF SOME GIRLS CAME ALONG
THERE'S NO HOPE

DOC BOY! OUR DATES ARE HERE!
EEEEEEK!
© 1984 United Feature Syndicate, Inc.
JIM DAVIS 11-24
CAN WE TALK?
CAN WE LAUGH?

JIM DAVIS 11-26
I WONDER WHO THAT COULD BE, DOC BOY
DING DONG
DAD! MOM! WHAT ARE YOU DOING HERE!?
WE MISSED YOU BOYS, OKAY?
© 1984 United Feature Syndicate,Inc.
A LITTLE PAINT, A FEW CURTAINS, A WOMAN'S TOUCH, THIS COULD BE NICE!
MY DAD, THE SENTIMENTAL FOOL. MY MOM, THE CLICHÉ

YOUR VISIT IS SUCH A SURPRISE, MOM. WHEN'S THE LAST TIME YOU AND DAD WENT OUT?
WE HAVEN'T BEEN OFF THE FARM SINCE '53
I DON'T BELIEVE THAT

GOOD HEAVENS! WHAT'S THIS?
THAT'S AN INDOOR TOILET, DAD

WOO-HA! AIN'T SCIENCE SOMETHIN'?
FLUSH
NOW I BELIEVE IT
JIM DAVIS 11-27

YOU AWAKE, JON?
OF COURSE NOT, DAD! IT'S 5 A.M.! WHAT ARE YOU DOING UP?
CLICK
11-28
© 1984 United Feature Syndicate, Inc

JPM DAVPS
I GOTTA MILK SOMETHING!
I'M LEAVING

YOU FORGOT THIS WHEN YOU LEFT HOME, DOC BOY
THANKS, MOM. I HAVEN'T SLEPT A WINK WITHOUT IT
WHATCHA GOT THERE, DOC BOY?
NOTHING! NOTHING! IT'S NOTHING!
11-29 JIM DAVIS
© 1984 United Feature Syndicate, Inc.
COULD IT BE A SHRED OF YOUR OLD BLANKIE?
CAREFUL WHAT YOU SAY ABOUT BLANKIES, FELLA

JIM DAVIS 11-30
UH, MOM... I WOULDN'T OPEN THAT IF I WERE YOU
EEEK!
© 1984 United Feature Syndicate, Inc.
SOMETHING IN THERE MOVED!
I'M SURE IT WAS JUST AN OPTICAL ILLUSION
GO AHEAD, TELL HER HOW THE LUNCH MEAT HAS EVOLVED INTO AN INTELLIGENT LIFE FORM

SO LONG, SON. WE GOTTA RUN. I MISS MY COWS
GIVE THEM MY BEST

SEE YUH, DOC BOY! THANKS FOR DECORATING MY HOUSE, MOM!
© 1984 United Feature Syndicate, Inc.
JIM DAVIS 12-1

HELLO... UNDECORATORS?
JON IS A MAN OF GOOD UNTASTE

GARFIELD, I'M GOING TO A CARTOONISTS' CONVENTION, AND THE MOTEL WHERE I'M STAYING WON'T ACCEPT PETS
JIM DAVIS
12-3

SORRY, ODIE. YOU CAN'T GO

GARFIELD, YOU ARE A PET
RATS! I KEEP FORGETTING
SNAP!

I'M LEAVING FOR THE CARTOONISTS' CONVENTION NOW, GARFIELD. THERE'S A WEEK'S WORTH OF FOOD FOR YOU
A WEEK'S WORTH, HUH?
GARFIELD
JIM DAVIS
12-4

GARFIELD

IT WAS MORE LIKE 11 SECONDS' WORTH
GARFIELD

I HOPE JON COMES BACK FROM THAT CONVENTION SOON
JIM DAVIS 12-5
I HOPE I CAN SURVIVE THIS WEEK ON MY OWN
CLICK
I HOPE THAT DOOR ISN'T LOCKED

WHAT A TRAGIC SCENARIO... "OWNER LEAVES FOR WEEK... CAT LOCKS SELF OUT OF HOUSE... CAT STARVES ON FRONT PORCH"
12-6
HEY, WAIT A MINUTE! I CONTROL MY DESTINY! I DON'T HAVE TO STARVE ON THE FRONT PORCH!
JIM DAVIS
© 1984 United Feature Syndicate, Inc.
"CAT STARVES IN BUSHES"

AS LONG AS I'M LOCKED OUT OF THE HOUSE, I GUESS I'LL STRIKE OUT IN SEARCH OF FOOD
GEE, THIS NEIGHBORHOOD DOESN'T LOOK FAMILIAR TO ME
© 1984 United Feature Syndicate, Inc.
OH, NO! WHERE AM I?!
JIM DAVIS
12-7

I GOTTA FIGURE A WAY TO MEET SOME CHICKS
JIM DAVIS 12-8
YOU GOT A PROBLEM THERE, GUY?
STRIKING MANLY POSES DOESN'T SEEM TO BE DOING IT

GARFIELD! I'M BACK FROM THE CONVENTION! WHERE ARE YOU, BIG GUY?... GARFIELD?!
12-10
OH, NO! THIS IS TERRIBLE! GARFIELD DIDN'T GET LOCKED OUT OR ANYTHING, DID HE, ODIE?
YUP
JIM DAVIS

HELLO, GARFIELD
DO I KNOW YOU?
© 1984 United Feature Syndicate,Inc.
LET ME GIVE YOU A HINT... SIT UP STRAIGHT. DON'T TALK WITH YOUR MOUTH FULL. WAKE UP, SLEEPYHEAD
12-11
JIM DAVIS
MOM!

IT'S GREAT SEEING YOU AGAIN, MOM
YES, IT'S BEEN A WHILE
12-12
JIM DAVIS

IT SEEMS LIKE ONLY YESTERDAY

THIS WAS YOUR FIRST BED
IT **HAS** BEEN A WHILE

MOM, I DON'T RECOGNIZE THIS PLACE. I THOUGHT I WAS BORN IN THE KITCHEN OF AN ITALIAN RESTAURANT
IT CLOSED YEARS AGO, DARLING
IT'S ALL GONE! WHERE'S THE PASTA? THE PEOPLE? THE PASTA? THE EXCITEMENT? THE PASTA?
YOU ALWAYS DID LOVE TO EAT
SNIFF... OLD HABITS ARE HARD TO BREAK
JIM DAVIS 12-13

FATHER, THIS IS YOUR GRANDSON, GARFIELD. HE WILL BE STAYING WITH US FOR A WHILE
JIM DAVIS
12·14

IF YOU'RE GOING TO STAY HERE, BOY, YOU'RE GOING TO BE A MOUSER LIKE THE REST OF US

SO THIS IS MY GRANDSON AND YOUR SON, HUH?
MAYBE THEY SWITCHED KITTENS IN THE MATERNITY WARD

IF I HAVE TO BE A MOUSER TO STAY HERE, GRANDPA, I'LL DO IT! I HAVE MADE A NAME FOR MYSELF IN THE MOUSING GAME
12-15
© 1984 United Feature Syndicate, Inc.
THEN EAT THAT MOUSE
ARRRGH!!! PLEASE! PLEASE DON'T MAKE ME EAT IT!
I'D RATHER SWALLOW MY PRIDE THAN THAT MOUSE
JIM DAVIS

GEE, I MISS HAVING GARFIELD AROUND. I EVEN MISS THE ABUSE
JIM DAVIS 12-17

RRR!

THANKS, ODIE, BUT IT JUST ISN'T THE SAME

I'D LOVE TO CATCH YOUR MICE, GRANDPA, BUT I HAVEN'T SEEN ANY WORTHY OF MY TIME. GOT ANYTHING BIGGER?
BRING ON THE TRAINING MOUSE!
JIM DAVIS 12-18
© 1984 United Feature Syndicate, Inc.
ME AND MY BIG MOUTH

I'M SORRY I CAN'T STAY, MOM
IT'S FOR THE BEST, DEAR. YOU'D BETTER HURRY HOME. IT'S ALMOST CHRISTMAS
JIM DAVIS 12-19

CHRISTMAS! I ALMOST FORGOT!

I ALSO FORGOT I'M LOST

WELL, THIS IS JUST GREAT. I'M COLD, I'M HUNGRY, I'M TIRED...
12-20 JIM DAVIS

IT'S SNOWING TO BEAT THE BAND, AND I HAVEN'T THE FOGGIEST IDEA WHERE I AM

WHILE EVERYONE ELSE IS HAVING A WHITE CHRISTMAS, I'M GOING TO HAVE A WHITE LOST

I'M COLD, I'M HUNGRY AND I'M TIRED
JIM DAVIS 12-21

THEY SAY, IN CASES LIKE THIS, YOU SHOULD FIGHT SLEEP

I SAY, WHY FIGHT AN OLD FRIEND?
FOOMP

GARFIELD! WAKE UP! YOU'RE NEAR HOME!
JIM DAVIS 12-22

HUH? MOM? WHA...?!

WOW... IT NEVER LOOKED BETTER

WHERE IS IT WRITTEN THAT HUMANS MUST GIVE CATS MILK IN SAUCERS?! WHY NOT IN CUPS OR BOWLS OR PANS?
8·17
JIM DAVIS
SPLASH!
SEE?!
I THINK GARFIELD IS TRYING TO TELL ME SOMETHING
© 1984 United Feature Syndicate, Inc.

WHAT IS IT, GARFIELD?
JIM DAVIS
PICK ME UP
TOO FAT TO HOP ON THE TABLE, HUH?
8·18
ONE OF THESE DAYS, I'LL LEARN
© 1984 United Feature Syndicate, Inc.

IT'S MONDAY MORNING. A COLD, GRAY, DRIZZLY MONDAY MORNING
9-24
JIM DAVIS
SOME DUDE WITH A TRUMPET IS WAILIN' SOME BLUES ON THE RADIO AND MY BREAKFAST IS COLD
GARFIELD
IT'S ALL SO PERFECTLY DEPRESSING I CAN'T WIPE THIS SMILE OFF MY FACE
GARFIELD
© 1984 United Feature Syndicate, Inc.

MUNCH
SMACK
SLURP
GARFIELD
9-26
UH-OH!
JIM DAVIS
© 1984 United Feature Syndicate,Inc.
QUICK-
FOOD

GARFIELD
9-27
BARK!
TWENTY YEARS FROM NOW I'M GOING TO LOOK BACK ON THIS AND LAAAAAAUGH
ROWR
FFFFT!!
JIM DAVIS

OH, COME ON, GARFIELD. THE CAT FOOD ISN'T THAT BAD
GARFIELD

THEN LET'S SEE HOW **YOU** LIKE IT!
GARFIELD

MMM GOOD
YOU LIE!
GARFIELD
9·29

THIS FEELS LIKE A GREAT DAY TO SPEND IN BED
JIM DAVIS
10-8

HOP UP, GARFIELD. WE'RE GOING ON A PICNIC!
GIVE THE BUGS AND SNAKES MY REGRETS. I AIN'T GOING

I'LL GET YOU FOR THIS, MONDAY!

WHAT'S THIS?
I PACKED THE MICROWAVE FOR OUR PICNIC
10-9
WELL, I'M LEAVING IT HERE
© 1984 United Feature Syndicate, Inc.
JIM DAVIS
WHA....!
IF THE TELEVISION STAYS, I STAY

WAIT 'TIL YOU TASTE MY CHERRY PIE, GARFIELD. IT'S THE WORLD'S BEST
JIM DAVIS
I AGREE
© 1984 United Feature Syndicate, Inc.
10-10
22 MILLION ANTS CAN'T ALL BE WRONG

THE PICNIC'S ALL SET, GARFIELD
JIM DAVIS
DID I FORGET ANYTHING ?
YOU FORGOT THE BRICK FOR THE TABLECLOTH
10-11

THAT PESKY WIND WON'T SPOIL OUR PICNIC NOW, GARFIELD
WHERE'S THE MUSTARD?
© 1984 United Feature Syndicate, Inc.
UNDER THE THIRD ROCK FROM THE LEFT
JIM DAVIS 10·12

WELL, GARFIELD, THE ANTS ATE MY CHERRY PIE. THE WIND BLEW THE FOOD EVERYWHERE
DON'T SAY IT! DON'T SAY IT!
WHAT ELSE COULD POSSIBLY GO WRONG?
© 1984 United Feature Syndicate, Inc.
YOU SAID IT!
JIM DAVIS
10-13

NO! NO! NO! DON'T MAKE ME DO IT!
ARRRGH! SOMEONE HELP ME!
JIM DAVIS 8-6
SOMETIMES IT'S HARD TO FIGHT PRIMAL INSTINCTS
© 1984 United Feature Syndicate, Inc.

HELLO, LUNCH
8-7
JIM DAVIS
THOSE BIRD'S NESTS ARE DECEPTIVELY LARGE

WHY DO I DO IT? WHY DO I CLIMB UP TREES WHEN I CAN'T CLIMB DOWN?
JIM DAVIS
8-8

THE NEIGHBORHOOD ALWAYS TURNS OUT TO SEE ME. THEN THE FIRE DEPARTMENT COMES TO GET ME. THEN MY PICTURE ENDS UP IN THE NEWSPAPER

I JUST ANSWERED MY OWN QUESTION

OH GOOD! HERE COMES A FIREMAN TO SAVE ME!
8-9
JIM DAVIS
TERRIFIC. WHY DO I ALWAYS GET THE FAT ONES?
© 1984 United Feature Syndicate, Inc.
AND THE ONES WHO ARE SENSITIVE ABOUT THEIR WEIGHT?

I'M GETTING SLEEPY
JIM DAVIS
8-10
IF BIRDS CAN SLEEP IN TREES, SO CAN I
© 1984 United Feature Syndicate, Inc.
Z

OTHER GARFIELD BOOKS IN THIS SERIES

No. 1	Garfield The Great Lover	£2.50
No. 2	Garfield Why Do You Hate Mondays?	£2.50
No. 3	Garfield Does Pooky Need You?	£2.50
No. 4	Garfield Admit It, Odie's OK!	£2.50
No. 5	Garfield Two's Company	£2.50
No. 6	Garfield What's Cooking?	£2.50
No. 7	Garfield Who's Talking?	£2.50
No. 8	Garfield Strikes Again	£2.50
No. 10	Garfield We Love You Too	£2.50
No. 11	Garfield Here We Go Again	£2.50
No. 12	Garfield Life and Lasagne	£2.50
No. 13	Garfield In The Pink	£2.50
No. 14	Garfield Just Good Friends	£2.50
No. 15	Garfield Plays It Again	£2.50
No. 16	Garfield Flying High	£2.50
No. 17	Garfield On Top Of The World	£2.50
No. 18	Garfield Happy Landings	£2.50
No. 19	Garfield Going Places	£2.50
No. 20	Garfield Le Magnifique!	£2.50
No. 21	Garfield In The Fast Lane	£2.50
No. 22	Garfield In Tune	£2.50
No. 23	Garfield The Reluctant Romeo	£2.50
No. 24	Garfield With Love From Me To You	£2.50
No. 25	Garfield A Gift For You	£2.50
No. 26	Garfield Great Impressions	£2.50

GARFIELD GALLERIES

Garfield Gallery No. 1	£4.95
Garfield Gallery No. 2	£4.95
Garfield Gallery No. 3	£4.95
Garfield Gallery No. 4	£4.95
Garfield Gallery No. 5	£4.95
Garfield Gallery No. 6	£4.95
Garfield Gallery No. 7	£4.95

GARFIELD COMIC ALBUMS

No. 1	Sitting Pretty	£3.99
No. 2	Words Of Wisdom	£3.99

COLOUR TV SPECIALS

Here Comes Garfield	£2.95
Garfield On The Town	£2.95
Garfield In The Rough	£2.95
Garfield In Disguise	£2.95
Garfield In Paradise	£2.95
Garfield Goes To Hollywood	£2.95
A Garfield Christmas	£2.95
Garfield's Thanksgiving	£2.95
Garfield's Feline Fantasies	£2.95
Garfield Gets A Life	£2.95
Garfield's Night Before Christmas	£3.95
Garfield's Tales Of Mystery	£3.95
Garfield's Scary Tales	£3.95
Garfield The Easter Bunny?	£3.95
Garfield Best Ever	£4.95
Garfield Selection	£5.95
Garfield His 9 Lives	£5.95
Garfield Diet Book	£4.95
Garfield Exercise Book	£4.95
Garfield Book Of Love	£2.99
The Garfield Birthday Book	£3.99

All these books are available at your local bookshop or newsagent, or can be ordered direct from the publisher. Just tick the titles you require and fill in the form below. Prices and availability subject to change without notice.

Ravette Books, PO Box 11, Falmouth, Cornwall, TR10 9EN.

Please send a cheque or postal order for the value of the book, and add the following for postage and packing:
UK including BFPO – £1.00 per order.
OVERSEAS, including EIRE – £2.00 per order.
OR Please debit this amount from my Access/Visa Card (delete as appropriate).

Card Number ☐☐☐☐☐☐☐☐☐☐☐☐☐☐☐☐

AMOUNT £ .... EXPIRY DATE ....

SIGNED ....

NAME ....

ADDRESS ....

....